The Irish Pope-Kings Formerly The

Rulers Of Britain

Conor MacDari

Kessinger Publishing's Rare Reprints

Thousands of Scarce and Hard-to-Find Books on These and other Subjects!

- Americana
- Ancient Mysteries
- Animals
- Anthropology
- Architecture
- Arts
- Astrology
- Bibliographies
- Biographies & Memoirs
- Body, Mind & Spirit
- Business & Investing
- Children & Young Adult
- Collectibles
- Comparative Religions
- Crafts & Hobbies
- Earth Sciences
- Education
- Ephemera
- Fiction
- Folklore
- Geography
- Health & Diet
- History
- Hobbies & Leisure
- Humor
- Illustrated Books
- Language & Culture
- Law
- Life Sciences

- Literature
- Medicine & Pharmacy
- Metaphysical
- Music
- Mystery & Crime
- Mythology
- Natural History
- Outdoor & Nature
- Philosophy
- Poetry
- Political Science
- Science
- Psychiatry & Psychology
- Reference
- Religion & Spiritualism
- Rhetoric
- Sacred Books
- Science Fiction
- Science & Technology
- Self-Help
- Social Sciences
- Symbolism
- Theatre & Drama
- Theology
- Travel & Explorations
- War & Military
- Women
- Yoga
- *Plus Much More!*

**We kindly invite you to view our catalog list at:
http://www.kessinger.net**

Because this article has been extracted from a parent book, it may have non-pertinent text at the beginning or end of it.

Any blank pages following the article are necessary for our book production requirements. The article herein is complete.

CHAPTER VI

THE IRISH POPE-KINGS FORMERLY THE RULERS OF BRITAIN

A WRITER in the *Encyclopædia Britannica*, in the article on Ireland, gives a very adroit presentation of when and how the Scots (Irish) were converted to Christianity. He seems to be conscious of the deception that has been perpetrated on the world and that the history of this event could be presented to us in an improved and more plausible fashion than it has ever been done. This deficiency he has endeavored to make up by cunningly mixing into his narrative, in a neat dress, a composition of some truth with fable and fiction. And all in such a manner as to make his story, to the uninitiated, appear like a very "fair" and truthful account. But, now that the truth is out, his story falls flat, although cleverly gotten up and evidently intended to be a very satisfactory summary of Ireland's past. As the *Britannica* is supposed to have weight, it appears to be a good medium for circulating such misleading information.

It is quite obvious that the object is not to tell the truth but to connect up all the better the missing links of the story which his predecessors might have been a little slack about in making it look "right." It would really be amusing if it were not so unjust to see how he tries to "mix up things" by trying to confuse the reader as to the identity of the Scots, the Picts, and the Southern Irish of Munster.

The truth is that they are all of one race and people, and these names have been given to them separately as a part of the scheme to confuse. The nearer to the seat of the great crime the greater the need to confuse any would-be investigators. This writer says: "At that time (314 A.D.) the Irish had possession of many places in west and south Britain, and must have come in contact with Christians. These were more numerous and the Church better organized in South Wales and Southwest Britain, where the Munster or Southern Irish were, than in North Wales which was held by the Scots proper" (*Encyclopædia Britannica*, 9th Ed., p. 247). This is an example of how he tries to confuse his readers by making it appear that there was easy intercourse between the Irish and Roman followers. There was no such intercourse. The adherents of each Church were practically identical with their armies. The Roman Church was only where the Roman spearhead was and nowhere else in Britain. Nor did the Romans lay claim exclusively to the title of "Christians" until, as is said, after 325 A.D., after the Council of Nice. And there was no moving about of the inhabitants from the Roman to the Irish lines. They were kept as much apart as the peoples of the French and German territories during the late World War.

There was no difference in race between the people of Munster, whom he calls Irish, and the same people whom he calls the "Scots proper in North Wales." And there

was no difference between those two peoples and the
Picts. They were all the same people and Eire or Arran
(called Scotia by the priests) was the motherland of the
race. The name of Scotia or Scotland has been trans-
ferred to Alba, as part of the deception. As there has
been a great crime committed and a monstrous imposture
put over on the people of the world, they found it to be
extremely necessary to write an account of those people
that would be confusing, and to change even the local
names of places. So those British priests have written
up a lot of mythical accounts of tribes and characters
with which to do this. It is very easy to see through
it when it is explained. But it requires study with the
necessary knowledge, at first, to understand it.

The accounts of the early beginnings as given in the
histories of Ireland, Scotland, and England, like the early
histories of other countries, were all written and composed
by the clergy, and for purposes of deception and for the
very reasons set forth in these pages. They have done
this work under assumed names in order to conceal the
fact. And what they have written is a concoction of
fiction and fable mostly, that is, so far as real, actual,
matter-of-fact happenings are concerned.

The priests who conceived the plan to deceive us, by
giving the name of Picts to a tribe of people, took as a
basis for their idea a class or order among the Ancient
Irish Priesthood of Iesa, who were ascetics. They have
called them a tribe and have given them the name of
Picts, just as if we today should call the Odd Fellows or
Bishops a different race from the rest of the American

people. The word "Pict" means a musician, and
is a camouflaged word for a Druid Priest or Magician,
one who understands sacred magic, or the occult spiritual
forces locked up within the human body. The body is
called the "lyre of Apollo" and he who understands that
instrument is therefore a pict or "musician," because of
certain nerve centers or ganglia through which the
spiritual force energizes. This is why the Harp is an
insignia of the ancient Irish and secretly alludes to
Ireland's distinction and preëminence as the homeland
of the. Magian Priesthood. No other country or people
has such a symbol, and for a good and sufficient reason.

The Irish, previous to the English invasion and the
sack of their church, were called Scots, we are told, not
"Irish" or "Picts," by the Romans. The island had
many names attesting to its spiritual character, but
Ireland was not one of them. This name is a living
testimony to British perfidy and cupidity, for they
conferred this name upon it.

That Ireland was preëminently the Sacred Isle of
"Spiritual" Sun worship, and not the Sacred Isle of
"Romanism," as the Roman priests would have us
believe, can be seen even by the very names of its
provinces. It is figuratively likened to a living being.
Ulster is the head or top of the island, and Munster is
the lowest point or foot; Leinster is the day or dawn
side, and Olnegmach or Connaught is the side on which
the Sun departs or the "nightside of the Sun," while
Meath represents the middle or midriff of the island, or
body.

This writer surely does try to make out that, because there were Roman Christians in Britain in the beginning of the fourth century, there were Roman Christians in Ireland. He cites the fact that there were British bishops at the Council of Arles in 314 A.D. If so, they most likely came from the British territory that had been conquered by the Roman arms and held for the Roman Church, so it is not surprising that they were there, for they were Romanists. None other would have been allowed to live in that territory. They must become Romanists or die. The Irish Church, which was the original Christian Church, was in a struggle for its very life with Rome, and it never surrendered or compromised. Hence, the war to the finish; and false statements, no matter how cunningly invented, cannot alter this fact. Rome has the stolen goods in her possession and she has falsified to the world as to where and how she obtained possession of them. They have set up, and quote from, many false authorities, but to no purpose.

The same writer says that the Irish held many places in West and South Britain about this time, and only legends would show an Irish occupation of a much earlier time (*Enc. Brit.*, 9th Ed., p. 246), and that they must have met many Christians there. Yes, they did come in contact with the Romanists at the sword's point, but not in the manner in which he would have us believe. I may ask, "What were the Irish doing in England at this time in the South and West?" They were there at that time just as they had been there from long ages before, and the Celtic race occupied those islands;

they were ruled by the Irish Pope-Kings who held the
Sovereignty of all those islands. They were in the
south and west of Britain at this time, because they were
already the occupants of the country and were attacked
there by the forces of the invading Roman armies who
had won the central parts of the country. This writer
surmises and builds up false premises on which to put forth
further misrepresentations, and he calls upon the writings
of other clerics to bear him out, such as "Germanus,"
"Lupus," "Palladius," "Patrick," and "Colgan," also
the "Book of Armagh" and "Probus," etc,, just so
much worthless material so far as bona-fide authority
or truth is concerned. People are not so credulous today.
Times have changed since the day when a Bishop could
stand up and tell the people that he had just received a
letter from Christ telling them that they must do certain
things, and not do other things, as did Eustis, Abbot
of Flay (quoted in Richard A. Proctor's *The Great
Pyramid*), who told his flock that he had found a letter
from Christ that morning on the altar forbidding them
to engage in activities on Sunday. Clerical writers, or
the bishops, think that they can still "put one over."

It is said that, among the Balkan peoples, the Wallach
(native of Wallachia) is the sharpest in a trade or barter
of any of the peoples there. He is so clever that the
others say that he was born three days before the devil.
But it can safely be said that the "Bishop" was born
three days before the Wallach. To illustrate — Wallachia is a rocky and mountainous country where Nature
has been parsimonious of her gifts to man. Therefore,

it is only by great industry and effort that the people are able to eke out a living from those stony hills. But the priest thrives there. He sees to that. There is a super-stition prevailing that it is an ill omen to hear a hen cackle at night. The best way to avoid evil effects from this is to bring the fowl to the nearest monastery as a gift. An Irish proverb runs: " If there is a hen or goose, it's on the priest's table it will be." Webster's Dictionary has it that "to deacon" is to cheat, and observation has justified the application of the term. "To bishop" surely means to lie, judging from all the fiction that has been given out under that head. The Bishop is not chosen for his piety or spiritual qualities, but because of his administrative ability, shrewdness, and business qualifications.

The more this writer in the *Encyclopædia Britannica* tries to explain things, the more he unwittingly proves that our facts are as stated, that Rome came to Ireland centuries later than is claimed and then only to usurp, absorb, and destroy. In explaining the status in the Irish Church of the Comarba or the co-heir of the Bishop, as inheritor of both the spiritual and temporal rights, privileges of the spiritual tribe or family, who might be a layman and possibly have sole power fall to himself, he says: "This singular association of lay and spiritual powers was liable to the abuse of having the whole succession fall into lay hands, as happened to a large extent in later times. This led to many misconceptions of the true character and discipline of the Irish Medieval Church " (p. 248).

Aside from the question of whether the office of bishop
should be filled by a clerical or a layman, if Rome established her church rule in Ireland about the beginning
of the fifth century, as she claims she did, and converted
the whole island through the mission of "St. Patrick,"
and "peaceably and without the shedding of a drop of
blood," it is very strange that the Irish people who were
so easily converted and who so readily adopted the
Roman religion and priests, and who, if this were so,
were immediately under the discipline of the Roman
Church, should prove so recalcitrant later and have
maintained this insubordination all through *medieval*
times when Rome is supposed to have full sway there,
having according to supposition established her church
rule there from five to six hundred years previously.
This story we maintain is composed of fiction without a grain of truth. In Rome's history, in dealing
with opposition either of a people or of an insubor-
dinate branch of the priesthood, has she been shown
to pursue a vacillating or tolerant policy? Quite the
contrary.

She did not show much toleration in her treatment of
the Huguenots. The massacre of St. Bartholomew will
attest to that. She was a demon of cruelty wherever
she had power. Did she coddle the Albigenses in the
south of France when they refused to subscribe to her
beliefs? The Papal Envoy, the Abbot Arnold, gave
instructions to the general of the papal army, when the
latter said he could not distinguish the heretics from the
faithful: "Slay them all. God will know his own."

And, in the course of a few years, there were slaughtered 180,000 souls.

So history itself refutes the claim that Rome was dominant or even present in Ireland and substantiates the claim that the Irish Church had its own rule during *medieval* times, previous to the English conquest. They have invented the pretext "to discipline" as an explanation for King Henry's invasion, but it is merely a "cloak" under which to conceal the purpose and act of conquest of the Irish Church. The Pontiff of the Irish at this time, 1172 A.D., was Galasius. Roman writers claim him as their own under the designation of primate and refer to him as the "saintly Galasius." His name bespeaks his office as the representative of The Sun, from Gal, bright, The Sun. The name is a true and perfect idiom and ideal of the Irish Church Sun worship of Iesa. It does not connect up at all with Rome. In the light of the knowledge which we have today the deception is most transparent. This conquest and its results were the most important events in the history of the Roman Church, and they have been fraught with consequence to mankind. They represent truly the triumph of Might over Right.

The writer in the *Encyclopædia Britannica* tries to make fact and fiction correspond. but without success. The writers of the church have ad no scruples in the matter of altering facts to accomplish their purpose, and did not hesitate to use deception. Wolsey visualized the future when he was Bishop of London, in addressing a convention of the clergy on the subject of the printing press, which was new at the time (1474 A.D.), when he said: "If we do not destroy this dangerous invention, it will one day destroy us" (*Bible Myths*, p. 438, by T. W. Doane). It is in spite of the clergy that light and knowledge have spread.

This writer, already alluded to, says that the differences which existed in the Irish Church, as compared to the Roman Church, were due to Ireland's "isolation" (*Enc. Brit.*, 9th Ed., p. 250). But Ireland was not isolated in those days. It is only since she came under English rule that she became "isolated." Before that time, up to and for long after the Punic Wars, she was the greatest commercial nation in the world, for she was the homeland of the "Phœnicians" (Irish). Their trading ships sailed on every sea, and it is logical to assume, as a natural consequence, that the traders and merchants of other countries also visited "Phœnicia." Ireland became isolated for the same reason that a highwayman kills his victim after robbing him, that there might be no one alive to give testimony against him. It has been the settled and most carefully studied British policy to isolate and misrepresent Ireland. We hope that, as the truth comes to light, Englishmen will be moved to make what amends are possible for the horrible mistreatment and oppression which have been inflicted upon that country. The Irish people have suffered untold misery through no fault of their own, but because they had what Rome coveted for her own power, a Savior, the Bible, and spiritual sovereignty in the Papacy. England was but a tool used by Rome in her striving to attain her end, namely, recognition as the *sole source of the "Divine Authority" on earth.*

The aforementioned writer refers, too, to the question of "Easter," which Rome has given as her reason for the so-called disciplining of the Irish Church. He tells us that it caused a great deal of trouble in the church but endeavors to leave the impression that it never got beyond the limits of a mere polemic affair, a matter of heated discussion. He tells a little of the truth also which will show, as herein claimed, that the Irish Church of Iesa Chriost was the great church of Europe.

He has prepared his ground in advance for this brief but partial admission by saying that these establishments in the countries named were set up by Irish priests who were Christian missionaries within the Church of Rome. He refers to "peculiarities" which the Irish Church had, but says that they were only survivals of what was general at one time throughout the Christian Church and, of course, "Puritan" Rome was shocked at those things. He does not tell what those peculiarities were, but it is a natural inference that they must have been horrible and immoral if Rome could not tolerate them. She does not seem, even in this enlightened day, to be shocked at what her priests have done in the Philippine Islands, in Mexico, or in South America. For that matter, we do not need to go outside of our own country to look for evidence of it. But it is not our purpose to treat on Roman corruption or immorality.

Here is what the *Encyclopædia* writer says on the fictitious alibi of Easter: "On the Easter question especially a contest arose which waxed hottest in England, and, as the Irish monks stubbornly adhered to their traditions, they were vehemently attacked by their opponents. This controversy occupies much space in the history of the Western Church and led to an unequal struggle between the Roman and Scotic clergy in Scotland, England, the East of France, Switzerland, and a considerable part of Germany, which naturally ended in the Irish system giving way before the Roman. The monasteries following the Irish rule were supplanted by or converted into Benedictine ones" (9th Ed., p. 250).

This writer has said much when he admits that the "Irish System" and the Irish monks, under Irish rule, which of course was the rule of the Irish Supreme Pontiff, were so far afield from Ireland as to be in Britain, Scotland, the East of France, Switzerland, and Germany. Even this far would take the Irish monks quite a distance inland into the continent of Europe and proves our statement that the Irish Church of Iesa was there. Is he trying to show that the Irish monks were the sole and only missionaries in those countries converting the people for the benefit of Rome? This seems to be his object. By his statement, the Irish monks would be the preponderant or greatest element in the Roman Church, and were doing a great deal of zealous work for Rome. This could not be so, for we know that Rome was in the field with hostile armies for centuries. This writer fails to tell us what the Romans themselves were doing all of this time. They were trying to crush the Irish Church. Were not the Romans making any converts at all for their church? Were they simply marking time and letting the Irish do the work of conversion for them? His argument is weak and its absurdity needs only to be pointed out.

When this "mere contest," which he would have us believe was all within the Roman Church and "waxed hottest" in England and the other countries mentioned, was settled, why is it that Rome did not make the same changes in Ireland at that time, where she claims to have been established for so long a period, that she made in England and in those other places? Ireland must have been the seat of the trouble. Why did she not change things there? The reason is obvious. She had not been established there, and this writer only makes her course and her guilt appear all the more conspicuous, so much so that all mankind can see it.

Rome, as has been said before, made war on the Irish Church established all over Europe, and, as she advanced with her armed forces, she took possession of the church property and compelled the people to come under her church dominion or be put to death. By forgeries and lies she has tried to make the world believe that these countries were "converted" by her missionaries.

We will let this apologist for Rome speak once more, when he tries to give a little acknowledgment to the Irish monks for what was done by the Irish monks of the religion of Iesa thousands of years before the time he speaks of. He spans a big gap of time and pretends that those Irish monks belonged to the communion of Rome, which, of course, is false; for Rome came in only later with armies to conquer those countries and, by persecution and death, drove out the Irish monks and their successors. Rome appropriated their labors and works and claimed their very virtues as her own. He employs the very same rule which he frowns upon in others, thinking that in this way he can give his story the appearance of being truthful. Rightly enough, he is familiar with Roman methods of substitution and her invention of "Saints" where no saints were. He has made such a creditable attempt at misrepresentation in the foregoing part of his article that he can afford to be "generous" and fair in giving the Irish monks credit; even he himself is misrepresenting the plainest truth.

He says: "Owing to this struggle, the real work of the early Irish missionaries in converting the pagans of Britain and Central Europe and sowing the seeds of culture there, has been overlooked when not wilfully misrepresented. . . . Thus, while the real work of the conversion of the pagan Germans was the work of Irishmen, Winifred or, as he is better known, St. Boniface, a man of great political ability, reaped the field they had sown, and is called the Apostle of Germany, though it is doubtful if he ever preached to the heathen" (*Enc. Brit.*, 9th Ed., p. 250).

This shows us what has been Rome's way of making changes and inventing substitutes for purposes of deception, but the plot is now exposed, I hope, in such plain manner that no one will be at a loss to account for the growth of the Roman Church and the cause of the Roman wars against Carthage and the countries of

Western Europe, such as France (Gaul), Spain (Iberia), Germany, and England.   It was to crush the Irish Church of Iesa and to obtain the Popedom and its accessory possessions, the *Supreme* Papacy, the Savior, and the Irish Bible.

This is the end of this publication.

Any remaining blank pages are for our book binding
requirements and are blank on purpose.

To search thousands of interesting publications like this one,
please remember to visit our website at:

http://www.kessinger.net